LIFE IN
A VICTORIAN
SCHOOL

PAMELA HORN

IMPORTANT DATES

1808 Establishment of the non-sectarian Royal Lancasterian Association (later the British and Foreign School Society) to promote elementary schooling.

1811 Establishment of the National Society for the Education of the Poor in the Principles of the Established Church (usually shortened to the National Society) – the main school provider pre-1870.

1833 First state grant of £20,000 is made for elementary education.

1833 The Factory Act states that working children aged 9 to 13 must attend school for 2 hours daily, increasing to 3 hours in 1844.

1839 The first two of Her Majesty's Inspectors of Schools are appointed.

1846 Introduction of the teachers' certificate examination.

1862 The Revised Code for elementary education introduced, initiating the 'payment by results' system and annual examinations.

1870 Elementary Education Act designed to provide a school place for every child.

1870 National Union of Elementary Teachers established.

1880 Compulsory attendance at school for children aged 5 to 10, and thereafter to 13.

1891 Free elementary education becomes available; a government grant of 10s (50p) a year is payable for each pupil in a public elementary school.

1893 Minimum school leaving age raised from 10 to 11.

1899 Establishment of the Board of Education to superintend matters relating to education in England and Wales.

1899 Minimum school leaving age raised to 12, although in some agricultural districts 11 is still accepted.

◄ A slate and slate pencil, the writing tools of Victorian schoolchildren.

➤ An old-style gallery school in London for infants, c.1900. The use of a gallery saved schoolroom space and kept the children under close observation.

AN ELEMENTARY EDUCATION

Education in Britain can be traced back to Roman times; great institutions such as the colleges of Oxford and Cambridge were developed in the 13th century; and by the time Henry VIII was on the throne a wider emphasis was being placed on education for privileged boys. In Scotland an Act of 1696 stated that each parish should provide a school building and finance a teacher's salary, but it was not until Victorian times that provision was made in England and Wales for every child – both boys and girls – to have an elementary school place, whatever their background. New buildings were constructed, changes made in educational administration, and comparisons drawn with developments in other European countries. As a result, literacy rates improved. When Queen Victoria ascended the throne in 1837, when the population of Britain numbered around 18 million, only just over two-thirds of all men marrying and just over half of the women could sign their name rather than having to make a mark; by 1901, the year of the Queen's death, more than nine out of ten of her subjects could sign their name when they married.

The content and scope of the schooling provided gradually extended and compulsory education was introduced for elementary school pupils between 1870 and 1880. This revealed the special needs of some children, such as the poor diet of pupils from deprived areas and the difficulties experienced by blind, deaf, and physically and mentally disabled children. The first tentative steps were taken to remedy these.

Older middle- and upper-class children, too, had a greater range of schools available to them and a wider curriculum developed to meet the country's growing professional and commercial needs. But it is the children from ordinary families, who attended elementary schools, where the changes had the biggest effect on Victorian Britain. When W.E. Forster, Vice-President of the Education Department, introduced the 1870 Elementary Education Bill in the House of Commons, he said: 'Upon the speedy provision of elementary education depends our industrial prosperity. It is of no use trying to give technical teaching to our artisans without elementary education … and if we leave our work-folk any longer unskilled, notwithstanding their strong sinews and determined energy, they will become over-matched in the competition of the world. Upon this speedy provision depends also, I fully believe, the good, the safe working of our constitutional system.'

The early aim of Victorian schools was to instil religious principles and moral values into the pupils. Religious instruction, and sometimes lessons in reading and writing, was something the Sunday Schools had sought to achieve for working-class children from the late 1700s but with limited success, given their restricted finances, inexperienced teachers and the limited time pupils attended. They did have the virtue, however, of being free, which did not apply to most elementary day schools. In addition they did not disrupt any work plans the children might have.

But while religion was important, throughout the Victorian era the general organization of schooling was essentially class-based, designed to fit children for the station in life into which they had been born. This affected all aspects of their school life, from the curriculum they followed to the length of time they attended, and the age at which they were expected to leave.

The general philosophy was expressed in 1867 by Robert Lowe, a former Vice-President of the Committee of Council on Education (in effect an Education Minister) when he declared: 'The lower classes ought to be educated that they may appreciate and defer to a higher cultivation when they meet it, and the higher classes ought to be educated that they may exhibit to the lower classes that higher education to which, if it were shown to them, they would bow down and defer.'

DAME SCHOOLS

The lack of a firm moral and religious message led to doubts about the role of the many small private 'dame' schools which had been set up by a variety of so-called teachers. Dame schools – usually run by elderly women, and sometimes men, of varying abilities – also offered instruction, especially to young children, but most were conducted in cottage

A DULL REGIME

Joseph Ashby of Tysoe, Warwickshire, attended the local National School in the 1860s and recalled its dull regime: 'Right up the school … you did almost nothing except reading, writing and arithmetic. What a noise there used to be! Several children would be reading aloud, teachers scolding, infants reciting … A specially hard time was the two sewing afternoons. While the girls were collected together for sewing, the boys merely did more sums or an extra dictation … Some boys couldn't get through a day without "holding out their hands" … One didn't learn much … School was so unreal. That explained the truancy and the caning and much else.'

rooms by a 'teacher' who combined her schooling with domestic chores. In 1871 it was reported that 53-year-old Maria Busby's school in Chelsea, London, was attended by eight boys and two girls, who were taught in Mrs Busby's kitchen, while she was 'carrying on mangling'. One girl, aged over 7,

▲ A Norfolk dame school in the 1880s.

▲ A variation on the dame school theme: pupils attending Mrs Dobbins's lace school at Stokenchurch, Oxfordshire, in 1860. The school trained youngsters for this cottage industry rather than instructing them in the three Rs – reading, writing and arithmetic.

➤ Religious influence continued to be exerted in education into the early 20th century. The rector, the Revd A.J. Wilson, is listening in to lessons at Tackley National School, Oxfordshire, in June 1905.

could read and another child could write, but clearly the education offered was minimal. Parents may have chosen it for its informality and its child-minding service, and were willing to pay the weekly fee of 4d or 5d (2p) she charged, rather than seek out a more efficient school.

In areas such as the South Midlands, where cottage industries survived, such as straw plaiting for the straw hat manufacturers and pillow lacemaking for the fashion trades, special craft schools existed where the children concentrated on these skills rather than on ordinary lessons.

RELIGIOUS INTERVENTION

The main elementary education provided in the early Victorian period was supplied by two religious bodies – the National Society, formed in 1811 by supporters of the Church of England, and the British and Foreign School Society, established in 1808 under its original name of the Royal Lancasterian Association and adopting its new name in 1814. It was ostensibly non-sectarian but in practice was supported by Nonconformists. Later, other religious societies were founded, such as the Wesleyan Education Committee in 1840 and the Catholic Poor School Society in 1847, each promoting denominational schooling. The Church of England was the most active and in 1860 it owned around nine-tenths of all public elementary schools and enrolled about three-quarters of the pupils.

▶ Ragged School dinner in Camberwell, London, c.1900. The Ragged School Union was formed in London in 1844 for destitute children and provided free education. Over 120,000 children in London were estimated to be underfed in 1904.

▲ A corrective institution. Boys in the sparsely furnished schoolroom at Hardwicke Reformatory School, Gloucestershire, in the late 19th century. The boys wore a rough corduroy uniform and heavy boots.

▲ Boys working in the school garden at Hardwicke Reformatory School, under the watchful eye of the Superintendent, William Robinson (wearing a boater), at the end of the Victorian era.

RAGGED SCHOOLS AND REFORMATORY SCHOOLS

For homeless and destitute children in large cities like London or Liverpool, their filthy condition and inability to pay fees led to their exclusion from the ordinary schools. Consequently in the 1840s charitably funded Ragged Schools were established to give them basic schooling and some notions of hygiene. Free meals, clothing, and craft training were supplied, the latter often being shoemaking and tailoring for the boys and domestic skills for the girls. The aim was to enable them to earn a living. By 1852, 41 towns (including London) had Ragged Schools.

For children who had committed crimes or were in need of care, residential reformatory and industrial schools were formed from the 1850s, to achieve their rehabilitation. Reformatories catered for those under 16 who had committed crimes punishable by imprisonment, while industrial schools were for under-14s guilty of minor offences or who had neglectful parents. Discipline was strict, and the education given was combined with vocational training and religious guidance. 'The children could expect hard labour, hard fare and a hard bed; treatment ... [was] directed mainly towards deterrence,' it was declared.

SCHOOL PENCE

Weekly fees known as the 'school pence' were levied, usually 1d or 2d (½p or 1p) from each pupil, although sometimes a sliding scale was applied, so that the offspring of farmers or tradesmen might pay 3d or 4d (1½ or 2p). Where families were large or fathers unemployed, paying the fees could prove difficult. Children were sometimes sent home to get their weekly pence, as at Grimsby Central Market Boys' Church School

▲ A Victorian penny.

in August 1863, when '26 boys [were] sent home to fetch their school pence'. Not until 1891 did an additional government grant make elementary education free for most – although not all – pupils. Occasionally a local benefactor paid the fees of particularly poor children, or the Poor Law authorities might do so. Sometimes children were kept away because they lacked footwear, as at Ampfield in Hampshire in October 1863, when one boy was absent for a week: 'no boots to wear'.

THE WORKING CLASSES

To the working classes, school was seen as an instrument of social control and moral reform at a time of national unrest, both politically and industrially, when there was a danger of youngsters growing up in ignorance. An official report of 1861 stated: 'A set of good schools civilizes a whole neighbourhood.' The intention was to create a disciplined and obedient labour force to meet the growing needs of industry and especially of factory production.

Yet public opinion was slow to abandon the view that, if necessary, working-class children should contribute to family income as soon as they were physically able, rather than attend school. As the 1861 Royal Commission on Popular Education commented: '… independence is of more importance than education; and if the wages of the child's labour are necessary, either to keep the parents from the poor rates, or to relieve the pressure of severe and bitter poverty, it is far better that it should go to work … than that it should remain at school.'

These attitudes limited the curriculum for working-class children to religion and the three Rs (reading, writing and arithmetic) plus needlework for the girls. Not until the 1870s and beyond was there an increase in the subjects studied by most elementary pupils.

RULES

To be observed by the Parents of Children attending the National

School at _____

Parents who wish to get their children admitted into the above-named school, may do so by applying to the Master on any Monday morning, at a quarter before 9 o'clock.

Parents are requested to pay particular attention to the following rules :—

1. The children are to assemble at the school on every week-day morning at a quarter before 9, and every afternoon at a quarter before 2 o'clock, except Saturday, which is a holiday.

2. On the Sunday the children meet in the morning at   , and in the afternoon at   o'clock.

3. The school hours are from 9 to 12, and 2 to 5, in the summer; and from 9 to 12, and 2 to 4, in the winter.

4. The children must be sent to school clean and neat in person and dress.

5. No child may stay from school without leave from the Master.

6. Leave of absence will be readily granted, either by application personally or by note: this application must be made before, and not after, the child absents itself.

7. If any child come late or be absent, a ticket of suspension will be sent, requiring a reason from the parent.

8. If the ticket be disregarded, the child will not be allowed to attend the school until a satisfactory answer has been given by the parent.

9. Every child must bring   a week, to be paid in advance every Monday morning: if there should be three children in one family desirous of attending the school, the third will be admitted free.

10. No child will be admitted under the age of six years.

N.B. No child will be admitted until it has been vaccinated.

Sold at the *National Society's Depository*, Sanctuary, Westminster.

▲ Rules of the National Society for its associated schools, from Lower Heyford National School, Oxfordshire, c.1867. Regular attendance, including at Sunday school, was expected, as well as being 'clean and neat in person and dress'.

In the early Victorian years the State played little part in elementary education. From 1833 a school building grant of £20,000 (the equivalent of around £1.5 million today) was divided between the National Society and the British and Foreign School Society, and was subsequently increased. In 1839 the first of Her Majesty's Inspectors of Schools (HMIs) were appointed, and from 1846 the State also gave financial support towards teacher training.

GOVERNMENT GRANTS

Until 1870 elementary schools were mainly provided by the voluntary organizations, supported by government grants, rising from £20,000 in 1833 to £669,000 by 1858 and leading to the appointment of a Royal Commission on Popular Education to investigate the effectiveness of the schools. From this came the 1862 Revised Code, which introduced a 'payment by results' system,

▲ Half-timers employed at a Farnworth mill in Lancashire, c.1900. The photograph was taken by Mr J.W. Pickford of the *Farnworth Journal*; he was a long-time critic of the half-time system.

THE THREE R's; OR, BETTER LATE THAN NEVER.

▲ The disputes and delays surrounding the passage of the 1870 Elementary Education Act are captured by this *Punch* cartoon of 26 March 1870. The Vice President of the Education Department is saying, 'Well, my little people, we have been gravely and earnestly considering whether you may learn to read. I am happy to tell you that, subject to a variety of restrictions, conscience clauses, and the consent of your vestries – *you may!*'

making government grants to elementary schools dependent on the pupils' attendance levels and their success in annual examinations conducted by the HMIs in reading, writing and arithmetic, plus needlework for the girls. These subjects were arranged in six standards, later seven, linking the child's age to the anticipated level of attainment. For the first time, an academic 'norm' was established for elementary pupils related to age and based upon a national curriculum. In 1867 new grants were offered for history, grammar and geography, and over the years other subjects, ranging from elementary science to singing, drawing and object lessons, were added. But they did not replace the three Rs as the core grant-earning subjects until 'payment by results' ended in the 1890s.

From 1862 head teachers also had to maintain a logbook to record the daily and weekly happenings at the school. The aim was to achieve accountability

HALF-TIME SCHOOLING

The 1833 Factory Act prohibited children under 9 years old from working in cotton and woollen mills; a system of half-time education was introduced, initially for children aged 9 to 13, limiting their working day to 7 hours and stating that they were to attend school for 2 hours a day. From 1844, children under the age of 8 could not work in textile mills, and from ages 8 to 13 they could work for 6½ or 7 hours a day and attend school for 3 hours, either in the morning or in the afternoon. Unless that happened the child could not work. Later the legislation was extended to other factories and workshops, and the 1867 Factory and Workshops Regulation Acts allowed no child under 8 to be employed in a handicraft.

and 'value for money' in elementary education. However, many pupils' irregular attendance and the deficiencies in teaching and equipment frustrated the anticipated progress of the children.

A NEED FOR MORE SCHOOLS

Nonetheless, by the late 1860s many voluntary schools had opened and most working-class youngsters attended for at least part of their childhood. Only a minority, living in urban slums or remote country districts, were still slipping through the net. Liverpool, Leeds and Manchester were three towns where provision lagged behind need, while in London in the early 1870s it was estimated that about a quarter of a million extra school places were required. To meet these shortfalls and to create a national network of efficient elementary schools the 1870 Elementary Education Act was passed. 'Had the state not intervened at this point,' wrote one commentator, '… the progress of literacy would have been considerably slowed … simply because illiteracy was by that time concentrated in those classes and regions that were hardest to provide for under the voluntary system of education.'

▼ The Revised Code of 1862 laid down the school curriculum to be followed in all state-aided elementary schools. It was introduced by the Vice President of the Education Department, Robert Lowe.

48.	Standard I.	Standard II.	Standard III.	Standard IV.	Standard V.	Standard VI.
Reading –	Narrative in monosyllables.	One of the narratives next in order after monosyllables in an elememtary reading book used in the school.	A short paragraph from an elementary reading book used in the school.	A short paragraph from a more advanced reading book used in the school.	A few lines of poetry from a reading book used in the first class of the school.	A short ordinary paragraph in a newspaper, or other modern narrative.
Writing –	Form on black-board or slate, from dictation, letters, capital and small, manuscript.	Copy in manuscript character a line of print.	A sentence from the same paragraph, slowly read once, and then dictated in single words.	A sentence slowly dictated once by a few words at a time, from the same book, but not from the paragraph read.	A sentence slowly dictated once by a few words at a time, from a reading book used in the first class of the school.	Another short ordinary paragraph in a newspaper, or other modern narrative, slowly dictated once by a few words at a time.
Arithmetic –	Form on a black-board or slate, from dictation, figures up to 20; name at sight figures up to 20; add and subtract figures up to 10, orally, from examples on black-board.	A sum in simple addition or subtraction, and the multiplication table.	A sum in any simple rule as far as short division (inclusive).	A sum in compound rules (money).	A sum in compound rules (common weights and measures).	A sum in practice or bills of parcels.

▲ A manual training centre at a London board school in the 1890s, when the rigours of the Revised Code system had been relaxed.

◄ The Church of England in Luton strongly opposed a school board. Not until 1874 did it finally admit it could not provide the additional school places needed. The first meeting of the new board took place in March of that year.

SCHOOL BOARDS

Under the 1870 Act every child was to be provided with a school place in a building of reasonable quality and with a qualified head teacher. The voluntary bodies were allowed six months to agree to meet any deficiency reported after a national survey of school facilities was completed. Only if they were unable or unwilling to 'fill the gaps' were new rate-aided, non-sectarian schools to be established, under the aegis of a board elected by ratepayers. The boards could impose compulsory attendance for children aged between 5 and 10 within their area, and thereafter to 12 or 13 according to local bye-laws, unless the youngsters could gain exemption or were working as half-timers. In addition, a 'conscience clause' allowed parents to withdraw their children from religious instruction in both board and voluntary schools.

Many voluntary school supporters, particularly those connected with Anglican schools, resisted the creation of school boards. Nonconformists, though, often favoured them since they did not want their children to attend a church school. The Bishop of Lincoln, a typical opponent, declared that every effort should be made to preserve denominational schooling: 'If the system of School Board teaching was spread widely he trembled for our civil and political institutions.'

Even when boards were elected time was needed to provide the extra school places required. In London, 98 temporary buildings were in use by July 1873 but more were still wanted. Many large towns resorted to rented accommodation.

SCHOOL BUILDINGS

Many early school buildings consisted of one big schoolroom for older pupils and a separate, smaller room for the infants. Also in towns it was common to provide separate rooms for boys and girls, with different entrances for each group and for the infants. However, in villages the entire school might be accommodated within one room. Occasionally temporary screens were erected between the classes, but they did little to reduce the noise as pupils undertook their different tasks, some reading aloud, others reciting poetry or chanting their multiplication tables. In larger urban schools, to maximize the use of space, long desks with fixed seating were provided in tiers, which almost imprisoned the children. At Tysoe, Joseph Ashby remembered the children being marched into the classroom and being instructed to put the left leg, followed by the right, over the seat before they sat down.

The walls of the classroom were covered with bare plaster, perhaps relieved by a few pictures, charts and maps. In summer the rooms became extremely hot and stuffy, and in winter the solitary stove or the one or two fireplaces proved insufficient to heat the room. Sanitary facilities were basic, with earth-closets, often evil-smelling, provided for the children's use in a small building across the school yard.

➤ Schoolroom interior with elaborate religious paintings on the wall. Few elementary schoolrooms were as ornate as this but the interiors tended towards an ecclesiastical appearance.

➤ A gallery-type London school in the 1890s. The pupils bending down on the left of the photograph are exercising with dumb-bells. In the older schools it was common to have a single large room for all the pupils.

A NEW PATTERN

After the establishment of the London School Board under the 1870 Education Act, however, improvements were introduced. Within three years of the Board's creation its architect went to Germany to study their buildings and returned with what became a standard pattern: instead of a single vast hall with tiered seats, he built separate classrooms which opened from the hall. This plan was subsequently adopted by school authorities nationwide, although in many rural areas the old single-room schools continued to be used. A commentator later referred to such new buildings as 'those solid, large windowed blocks' which gave thousands of children 'their first glimpse of a life of cleanliness, order, light and air'.

By the end of the century pianos and libraries had also been introduced in many of the town schools, so whereas in 1880 just over 2,000 schools had their own libraries, by 1895 that had reached nearly 6,400. In some more ambitious urban schools, rooms were set aside for science, cookery and handicraft classes, such as carpentry.

TEACHERS' HOUSING

From 1843 a state grant was made available for the building of teachers' houses. 'The schoolmaster,' a government minister declared in 1844, 'ought

▲ St James's School in Dudley was built in 1842. Boys aged 7 and over were taught in one half of the building, and girls and infants in the other, until the two were amalgamated in 1868. It functioned as a school until 1980 and is now part of the Black Country Museum.

to be provided with … a house, by no means too large, so as to exalt him too much in the scale of society; but he should be taken out of a cottage and put into a decent residence … calculated to make persons lower than himself, inclined to show a proper feeling of respect.' That was not always achieved, but many teachers' houses were built adjacent to the school itself, especially in villages. They varied in size but some were large enough to accommodate a pupil-teacher as well as the master or mistress's own family, if the young apprentice came from a distance away. In towns, however, teachers might have to rent a house or rooms, perhaps receiving a supplement to their salary to cover the cost.

CAUSE FOR COMPLAINT

'It is a lamentable fact, that many teachers' houses are a mere make-shift, as if anything was good enough to be inhabited rent free … In many places the three or four rooms constituting the house are under the school; in some places it forms one of a row of labourers' cottages … There may be some school-managers who imagine that I wish teachers to have mansions provided for them; not so, but build your teachers' houses as you would, at least, for a tenant of the middle class … you will thus cause the parents of the children to be duly impressed with the importance of your teacher's worth, and of his fitness for it.'

A correspondent to the *School and the Teacher*, January 1855

In the early part of the 19th century, even schools in more favourable districts were often overcrowded and staff insufficient. The teacher shortage was initially overcome by recruiting child monitors to assist, with the teacher instructing these older pupils. The monitors then passed on the information to younger schoolmates. Rote learning was the norm and not surprisingly the monitorial schools were soon condemned as sadly inadequate. Even the teachers were criticized in many cases, since few were formally trained. In 1845 it was said of Derbyshire schools: 'If the village school master be worse paid than the village carpenter or blacksmith, what hope is there of finding any but the most incompetent persons in the former situation?'

To counter this, from the 1840s teacher training colleges were set up, mainly by the Church of England and partly aided by government grants. From 1846 an apprenticeship system was introduced, whereby approved pupils from the elementary schools were apprenticed at age 13 (later raised to 14) for five years as pupil-teachers. They were instructed by the school head and had to pass annual examinations. In return, they received a small annual salary and were expected to help with the teaching at the school. For some, given the large size of many urban schools and the unruly character of some of the children, that proved daunting. If they completed the apprenticeship satisfactorily, they could sit a scholarship

∧ A school group at Marhamchurch, Cornwall, c.1900. A pupil-teacher is seen on the left, wearing a white pinafore.

➤ Teacher training colleges helped to raise the status of elementary teachers. Frances A. Goodway graduated from Stockwell Training College, London, in the mid-1890s. Born in 1874, she was the daughter of a coach builder in Banbury, Oxfordshire, and became head of Cherwell Infants' School, Banbury, from 1898 to 1927.

OVERCROWDED CLASSROOM

At the newly opened girls' school at Cinderford, Gloucestershire, in January 1878, the headmistress, an assistant teacher and a pupil-teacher had to cope with an intake of 157 children. There were not enough desks and, unsurprisingly, the head complained that it was 'very difficult to work the school in such a crowded state'.

▲ The teacher stands by the blackboard as the children participate in a 'free-arm' drawing class at Rosendale Road Board School, London, in 1897.

➤ A teacher's agreement at Kettering British School, Northamptonshire, in 1876. The teacher's salary depended in part on the pupils' success and attendance record at the annual school inspection, and thus on the amount of government grant earned by the school.

examination which gave entry to one of the teacher training colleges. Alternatively, they might continue in the schools as uncertificated assistants or, from 1847, they could take the teacher's certificate examination as an external candidate. In this way teaching standards were gradually raised and the status of teachers enhanced.

DISCIPLINE

Often, especially in large urban schools, teachers resorted to the cane to maintain discipline. Daisy Cowper, who attended a Liverpool church school in the 1890s, called her headmistress an 'ogress' who hit her hand so hard that she thought it would fall off. Occasionally parents retaliated in support of their children by physically attacking the teacher.

In addition to caning, punishments included keeping children in at the end of the day, something they hated, or, as at Cottisford school in Oxfordshire, making them stand in the corner with their hands on their head.

NATIONAL UNION OF TEACHERS

The National Union of Elementary Teachers was established in 1870, dropping 'Elementary' from its title in 1889. Aims of the Union in the mid-1890s included: 'To raise teaching to the dignity of a Profession by means of a Public Register of duly qualified Teachers for every class of Schools' and 'To establish a Scheme, whereby retiring allowances may be secured to aged and incapacitated Teachers.'

The purpose of the 1870 Elementary Education Act was to bring into school youngsters who had never before attended. It led to what one HMI called a 'large influx of rough and ragged children', and for their teachers it could mean dealing with mutinous youngsters who came only because they were compelled. They neither knew their alphabet nor were aware of basic habits of cleanliness, punctuality and discipline. Their attention span was minimal and even sitting still was a challenge. Many were malnourished or had skin complaints that distracted them. Better-off families were unhappy about their offspring associating with ragged, dirty and foul-mouthed fellow pupils. Consequently some school boards, like London, adopted a system of differential fees. This allowed an artisan rate-paying father to opt for a higher-fee school, secure in the knowledge his offspring would not come home 'harbouring lice from the children of the poorest' or learning the bad language of what one inspector called 'young blackguards swept in from the gutters'.

ABSENTEEISM

Attendances were often unsatisfactory, with parents keeping their children away because they could not afford the school pence or wanted them to work. Sometimes children truanted if they were punished,

EDUCATION.

Inspector of Schools. "IT STRIKES ME THAT TEACHER OF YOURS RETAINS LITTLE OR NO GRASP UPON THE ATTENTION OF THE CHILDREN,—NOT HOLD ENOUGH, YOU KNOW,—NOT HOLD ENOUGH—"

Lancashire Magnate (who takes great interest in the Educational Movement). "NOT HOLD ENOUGH! LOR' BLESS YER—IF SHE EVER SEES FORTY AGAIN, I'LL EAT MY 'AT!!"

▲ A *Punch* cartoon of a magisterial H.M. Inspector. In the 'payment by results' era HMIs had great power in assessing the success or failure of a school and its teacher.

◄ Rules to be observed by pupils and parents at Downton Free School, Wiltshire, in 1842 stated that the children 'are expected to enter the School-room in an orderly manner'. The parents were instructed 'not to encourage their Children in misbehaviour'.

DOWNTON FREE SCHOOL.

RULES TO BE OBSERVED BY THE CHILDREN AND THEIR PARENTS.

THE CHILDREN

1. Are to attend the School regularly at a quarter before Nine o'Clock in the Morning, and remain till Twelve. They are to attend also at half-past One o'Clock in the Afternoon, and from Lady Day to Michaelmas to remain till half-past Four o'Clock, and from Michaelmas to Lady Day till Four o'Clock.

2. They are to attend the School twice every Sunday at the appointed hours, and proceed with their Master to Church, both Morning and Afternoon.

3. They are to attend the School clean, washed, and combed.

4. They are not to absent themselves from the School without leave previously obtained from the Master. Those who do not comply with this Rule will be liable to punishment, and those who repeatedly offend against it will be dismissed altogether.

5. Each Child shall pay to the Master, in advance, one penny on every Monday morning, towards providing Books, Pens, Ink, &c.

6. They are expected to enter the School-room in an orderly manner, to behave at all times with respect, attention, and obedience to the Master and the Teachers, and on leaving the School to return home quietly, and not in any way to annoy or ill-treat their schoolfellows or any other persons.

THE PARENTS

1. Are to apply to the Trustees, or to the Subscribers, or to the Master, for a recommendation of their Children to be admitted to the School. In the admission of Children, a preference will be given to those who have not the means of otherwise procuring the benefit of instruction. Children will not be admitted before they are five years of age.

2. They are not to detain their Children from School without first assigning a reason to the Master, either in writing or in person.

3. They are not to remove their Children from the School without the consent of the Master, or of the Subscriber who recommended them.

4. They are not to encourage their Children in misbehaviour; but any Parent having a complaint to make, or any thing to state relative to the School, must apply to the Trustees or Subscribers; and will not, on any account, be allowed to enter the School for that purpose, unless expressly sent for.

5. They will be expected to keep their Children in good order at home; to set them a good example in all points of duty; and to further the work of domestic instruction as far as lies in their power, by assisting them in learning their lessons, by instructing them to read a portion of the Holy Scriptures, especially on the Lord's-day, and by using prayers every morning and evening in their families, so that both Parents and Children may have a better hope of obtaining the blessing and favour of God.

N.B.—The periodical Holidays to be allowed will not exceed one week at Christmas, one week at Whitsuntide, and one month during the harvest.

[W. B. HALPIN AND CO., HERALD OFFICE, SALISBURY.]

▼ Children from Fobbing Lane Church School, Essex, at the time of Queen Victoria's Golden Jubilee in 1887. The mistress was a Miss Milne and the little girls, who are wearing pinafores, have very short hair in many cases, probably to prevent the spread of nits.

▲ The benefits of thrift were inculcated at an early age at this London board school, where children are putting their savings in a post office account at the school. The post office encouraged young savers by allowing teachers to collect the pennies either by using stamps or by setting up penny banks.

or because they wanted simply to 'mooch about', as a Bristol pupil admitted. Furthermore, the compulsion clause in the 1870 Act only applied to school board areas. Not until 1876 were attendance committees formed in the rest of the country. Even then some failed to draw up the necessary bye-laws, so it was only in 1880 that compulsory attendance applied to all elementary pupils up to the age of 10 and thereafter to 13, unless they could gain exemption by passing a leaving examination or in some other way, such as achieving a high level of attendance over the preceding years. In 1893 the minimum leaving age was raised to 11 and in 1899 to 12, although in certain rural areas 11 was still accepted.

Good attendances were crucial to maximize a school's grant-earning capabilities. Furthermore, when children attended irregularly they learnt only 'by snatches' and were unable 'to gain sufficient grasp of any subject to retain it'. Some absences were unavoidable because the children were ill.

GOOD ATTENDANCE

Pupils were 'bribed' to go to school regularly by the offering of prizes for good attendance or for success in the annual examinations conducted by H.M. Inspectors. The London School Board even offered medals for good attendance throughout the year. Walter Southgate proudly recalled that he had obtained seven of these, 'and the seventh was considered a "gold" one'. Elsewhere special treats were organized as a reward.

At Whitchurch near Reading, Berkshire, early in 1886, a measles epidemic was followed by scarlet fever and then whooping cough. Even milder ailments like chilblains kept some children away because they 'can't get their boots on'.

Employment was a further cause of absenteeism. In country districts children acted as cheap labour on farms, weeding, planting seeds and helping at harvest, or looking after young siblings while

TRUANTS' MISDEMEANOURS

12 May 1882: Fred Oliver was summoned again before the magistrates today, for non-attendance (21 times out of 83). This is the 4th time and the case was again dismissed on Mrs Oliver's promise of sending him more regularly.

14 July 1882: James Kimber has been employed for the last 10 weeks illegally, also his brother ...

26 November 1882: Edward Nash (a habitual truant player) has been locked in the school by his mother's wish each dinner hour for the past 2 weeks. He has brought his dinner with him, and has been fetched at 4 o'clock. He is by no means a boy of bad disposition, but has been led away by boys who idle away their time in the streets.

Entries in Overton National Boys' School Log Book, Hampshire Record Office

their mother worked. In the towns youngsters ran errands, sold newspapers and other goods on the streets, and assisted around the home. In 1899 a London survey of 112 schools revealed that around two thousand pupils worked from 19 to over 40 hours a week in shops, factories and casual labour out of school hours. Most earned a paltry penny (½p) or so an hour, and when they got to school they were too tired to learn. In large towns, too, families often moved house frequently, in search of work or to escape the rent man, which disrupted their children's schooling. Similarly in factory districts, where half-timers often attended a school selected by their employer, if they went to another mill or the employer chose a different school, his young workers had to move on.

DEALING WITH TRUANTS

The school boards could appoint attendance officers to check up on truants. A number of large towns did so: in London officers were known as 'visitors', and in Bradford as 'persuaders'. Many families resented their advent and John Reeves, an attendance officer in the Shoreditch and Bethnal Green areas of London, recalled parents standing at the street door and hurling abuse 'in the most dreadful language, and nearly all the people in the street would … sympathise in their view'. In some parts of London the officers worked in pairs for protection. But even when children truanted

▼ A London School Board attendance officer – called a visitor – questions a truant in this posed photograph.

persistently and came before the magistrates for breaching the attendance bye-laws, they often escaped a penalty, or were fined such tiny amounts that they were no deterrent.

Yet, although by 1900, with the population of Britain at around 37 million, the scope of elementary schooling had widened and 5.7 million pupils now attended elementary classes, they were still seen as intended for society's 'lower orders' only, rather than the community at large.

THE SCHOOL DAY

A large bell suspended from the roof of the building summoned the children to school at 9am. Usually the day began with the singing of a hymn, often followed by a half-hour scripture lesson. Then there were ordinary lessons, divided into half-hour segments, in reading, writing, arithmetic and spelling. One Victorian schoolgirl, Kate Edwards, remembered that after prayers the children would get out their slates and begin practising their letters with a squeaking slate pencil: slates were cheap and could be wiped clean and reused, unlike paper. 'After writing we gathered round a big reading sheet and read from it, one word or sentence each,' recalled Kate. 'We used to sing songs because we had to get them ready for the day "the inspector" come … We had a lot of "po'try" for the inspector as well.'

There was no morning or afternoon break, but the midday break usually lasted for an hour and a half, so that some of the children could go home for their meal. Others brought bread and cheese or lard and ate in the classroom. They could then go out to play until afternoon school began, again signalled by the ringing of the bell at 1.30pm. Lessons continued until the school day ended at 4.30pm.

A WIDENING CURRICULUM
Gradually the scope of elementary schooling after 1870 was widened. Especially among older children in large urban schools, the curriculum was expanded to include science, history, geography and grammar, as well as music, drill, drawing and craft training, or domestic subjects for the girls.

◄ The bell on the former Factory School at Saltaire, Yorkshire, opened in 1868. Saltaire was a new town built by Sir Titus Salt for his employees, where children were 'only allowed to work half time at the mill and for the rest are sent to school'.

At Maud Clarke's Staffordshire school around 1900, the girls did not learn history or geography, though cookery, dressmaking and domestic science were included as they were considered appropriate for their future adult life.

History and geography lessons were influenced by the upsurge in imperial pride, especially during the South African War of 1899–1902. Some schools even displayed wall maps showing the progress of the conflict, and many pupils shared in the enthusiasm. Walter Southgate at Mowlem Street School in Bethnal Green recalled that he and his friends played games like 'English versus Boers', and exuberantly celebrated major military successes.

SPORTS AND GAMES
The opportunity for sports and games on school premises was lost to elementary pupils, mainly due to a shortage of cash and the curricular demands

◄ Assembly at a large London board school for girls c.1899. Many of the pupils are dressed in clean, white pinafores.

◄ Pupils performing drill exercises at Rosendale Road Board School, London, in 1897. Drill was introduced to elementary schools in the 1870s.

▲ Children from Ovington School, Hampshire, with their May garlands in 1895. The poverty of some of these children from farm labouring families is only too apparent, even though this was intended as a day of celebration.

▲ A Sunday school outing at Long Marston, Buckinghamshire, at the end of the Victorian era. Children stayed away from school to attend such treats.

of the Revised Code system. Drill and gymnastics were introduced on a small scale from 1871, and more widely during the South African War at the end of the century. Swimming in municipal baths was taken up by some town schools when special low entrance fees for pupils were negotiated. By the 1890s, as 'payment by results' was phased out, some elementary schools provided cricket and football grounds for the boys.

DAYS OUT AND CELEBRATIONS

The phasing out of 'payment by results' from 1890 made further changes possible, with some town schools taking pupils to visit museums and exhibitions; in country districts there was cottage gardening. In the summer of 1900, the head of a school in Overton, Hampshire, took over 40 boys on a day trip to Bournemouth where they enjoyed a boating pool, a 'good dinner', bathing, donkey rides and a walk around the town.

Some children had time off to attend Sunday school anniversary teas but for many pupils their principal pleasures lay in celebrating traditional festivals such as May Day, when they paraded with May garlands, or attending Christmas treats organized by well-wishers, when a lavish tea and gifts of toys and fruit might be provided. As one young girl summed it up: 'Living where we did and how we did, we used to make the most of anything a bit out o' the ordinary, and we looked for'ard from one special day to the next.'

PLAYTIME

School playgrounds were usually too small for all the children to play in before lessons began or at the end of the day, so they would stray on to the roads and town streets. The boys had games of marbles or played football using inflated pigs' bladders or old tin cans. The girls skipped with odd lengths of rope, perhaps part of a mother's old washing line, and enjoyed traditional singing games like 'Oranges and Lemons' and 'Here We Go Round the Mulberry Bush'. Both boys and girls had whips and tops, bowled hoops and played hopscotch and leapfrog. Toys were often home-made: a Norfolk girl remembered her father putting hobnails in the base of her top, which he had shaped from a large cotton reel.

SUFFER THE LITTLE CHILDREN ...

▲   The spread of elementary schooling after the 1870 Education Act revealed the inadequate diet of many impoverished school children. Here some youngsters in London queue for free meals.

➤   Children from Wigan, Lancashire, on 28 July 1893 at a soup kitchen in St Andrew's parish, when 6,000 colliers were on strike and relief committees were set up. The Chief Constable opened a soup kitchen to feed the strikers' families. The dispute ended in November 1893.

The large numbers of malnourished and ill-clad youngsters brought into the schools for the first time in the 1870s highlighted the prevalence of child health problems. This applied not only to urban slums, where children lived in overcrowded, insanitary homes, but also to country districts and the offspring of poorly paid farm labourers.

SCHOOL DINNERS

Teachers realized that many youngsters in the poorest areas were too malnourished to concentrate. As late as 1889 it was estimated that an eighth of pupils attending London elementary schools came to lessons hungry. It was in these circumstances that a number of charitable school meals schemes were established, one of the first in 1874 by Mrs Burgwin, the headmistress of Orange

Street Girls' School in Southwark. She was struck by the pale faces and listlessness of her pupils and was told by a medical friend this was because they were starving. At first Mrs Burgwin provided the children with bread and a hot drink but soon a local organization was created to provide regular free meals. In the early 1880s it won the support of George R. Sims, a campaigning journalist, who helped boost funds by publicising the work in the *Referee* newspaper. By the end of the century the 'Referee fund' was the largest single charity supplying free school meals in the capital.

At Nichol Street Board School in Bethnal Green, another area of desperate poverty, Lady Jeune took the lead. Not only were free meals provided for pupils during the winter but also free boots and clothing. She even arranged for children from both the boys' and girls' schools to go on free country holidays. By the end of the century there were six major charities in London offering free or cheap meals to needy children. Similar initiatives were taken in other towns. The Birmingham Schools Cheap Dinner Society, formed in 1884, soon discovered that many scholars were so poor they 'could no more find a halfpenny for a dinner than they could find a half-sovereign'. However, the availability of the schemes was patchy, with children in country areas losing out, as did those in towns like Sheffield and Liverpool where there was little or no provision.

Bread and soup were the mainstay of the dinners as they were easy to serve and were not so attractive that they appealed to the less needy. Yet, despite the limitations of the schemes, they paved the way in the post-Victorian era for rate-aided school meals to be provided, and in 1906 the Provision of School Meals Act was passed.

CHILDHOOD ILLNESSES

Illness represented a more serious challenge. Few remedies were available and the only recourse was to exclude children who were in contact with infections. In London an 1883 rule stated that pupils who had had diphtheria, scarlet fever, smallpox or typhus must stay away from school for two months, unless they had a doctor's certificate confirming they had recovered. Subsequently other childhood diseases were added to the list and in 1882 the Education Department laid down that schools should be closed entirely when a serious epidemic occurred among the children, as happened at Ampfield in Hampshire when the school was shut for a month in January 1884 because of a measles outbreak.

In 1890 the London School Board appointed a part-time medical superintendent to examine the children. Three years later Bradford followed suit,

appointing Dr James Kerr. He visited the schools and identified individual health problems. Thus in 1899 out of almost 300 children examined at one school he found that over a third had not had their clothes off for six months or more. This created skin complaints, and as a result fumigating stations were set up to free the clothing from vermin. A charity, the Cinderella Club, provided fresh clothes where necessary.

It was also reported that half-timers from Bradford mills were so exhausted by their work that they fell asleep in class. This was a common experience among factory children, and where they operated dangerous machinery tiredness could lead to serious injury, as at one Bolton mill in 1894 when a young cotton worker lost most of her arm in an accident.

SPECIAL SCHOOLS

One beneficial effect of the 1870s education legislation was that it gave a modest boost to the schooling of disabled children. Since all

▲ Orange Street School for infants in Southwark in 1894. This was a deprived area of London where charitable free meals were provided for local pupils from the 1870s.

HALF-TIMER IN A COTTON MILL

Children who held down jobs were often so exhausted that they fell asleep in class. In his *Memoirs 1869–1924*, J.R. Clynes described his working life as a half-timer in a cotton mill: 'Often the threads on the spindles broke as they were stretched and twisted and spun. These broken ends had to be instantly repaired … That was my job. I performed it, unresting, in my bare feet, since leather on those oil-soaked floors would have been treacherous. Often I fell, rolling instinctively and in terror from beneath the gliding jennies, well aware that horrible mutilation or death would result if the advancing monsters overtook and gripped me. Sometimes splinters as keen as daggers drove through my naked feet, leaving aching wounds … Running in and out, straining my eyes in the gas-lit gloom to watch for broken threads, my ten-year-old legs soon felt like lead, and my head spun faster than the pitiless machinery. But I had to keep on ….'

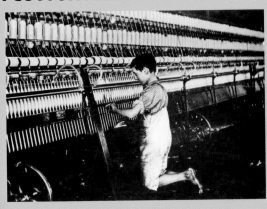

▲ A 'little piecer' working on a spinning mule at an Oldham mill in Lancashire, c.1900. A piecer's job was to mend broken threads on the machinery, an often dangerous task.

▲ Boys learning to make shoes at the Essex Industrial School and Home for Destitute Boys, c.1900. This was the darker side of school life, with firm discipline the order of the day.

youngsters were covered by the 1870 Act, as early as 1874 the London School Board opened its first class for deaf children and followed this in 1875 by a class for the blind. The example was gradually followed elsewhere, so that by the late 1880s five school boards in England and Scotland were educating blind children, and ten school boards taught deaf pupils. For those with learning difficulties, in some places special 'Standard O' classes were set up, where it was accepted that children could not meet the demands of the 'payment by results' system. However, most mentally disabled children remained outside the mainstream of elementary schooling or clogged up the lowest standards of the ordinary schools, irrespective of their age.

Yet, despite these deficiencies, the introduction of compulsory schooling highlighted the need to tackle child welfare issues on a national scale.

Oxfordshire's Abingdon School in 1874. Four years earlier it had moved from its cramped 16th-century site to a new location. At the time of the move this endowed grammar school had 45 pupils, 41 of whom are shown on the photograph.

When the Victorians referred to post-elementary schools they normally spoke not of secondary education but of 'middle-class' schooling. This underlined the fact that 'class' was still a major consideration in educational provision, and the system related to social status, parental occupation and family income.

In the first half of Queen Victoria's reign, middle-class education for boys included a mixture of ancient endowed grammar schools, proprietary schools established by companies or individual philanthropists, and private schools owned by the masters who ran them. They varied greatly in quality, giving rise to a growing concern at government level about the inadequacies of the system. There was anxiety, too, that the curriculum in many of the schools, by concentrating on the classics – Greek and Latin, was failing to respond to the country's industrial and commercial requirements.

From the 1850s a reform process began. First, a new breed of headmaster took over some of the less efficient grammar schools. Second, in 1858, Local Examinations for middle-class boys not intending to go to university provided a useful school-leaving qualification. Third, and most importantly, in 1864 the government appointed a Schools Inquiry Commission to investigate the whole of the non-elementary and non-public school sector. The Commission's 1867 report divided the schools it examined into three main groupings.

FIRST, SECOND AND THIRD GRADES

At first-grade schools, pupils normally stayed on to 18 or 19 years of age before proceeding to university. Their curriculum was much like that of the public schools, with an emphasis on the classics and mathematics. Where a 'modern' side was established, to meet the wishes of parents desiring their sons to follow a professional, business or military career, it often became the refuge of less able boys. Inevitably that devalued it in parents' eyes. Another adverse influence was that most families wanted their sons to have the opportunity to attend university, and for that proficiency in classics was essential. Schools within the first-grade category were patronized by the landed gentry, well-to-do professional men and industrialists. Some, like the public schools, also had boarding facilities.

An 1889 *Punch* cartoon of a middle-class school which concentrated on the classics. The headmaster is criticizing the boy whose Greek grammar is not as good as that of his younger brother. The 'dunce' responds, 'Ah, but my brother's not been here so long as I have, Sir. It's only his first term!'

Abingdon School fours in 1870. The school boat club was one of the oldest rowing clubs on the River Thames and was flourishing as early as 1840.

Second-grade schools were those where the boys' education normally ceased at around the age of 16 or 17. The lad concerned would then perhaps enter a family business or an office, or become apprenticed to what the 1864–67 Commission called 'all but the highest branches of the medical and legal professions' and engineering. Latin was still taught in these schools, partly for prestige and partly because it was thought to improve intellectual development, but other subjects were included as well, though not always sufficiently to please parents.

Finally, the Commission reported on what it labelled third-grade schools, where pupils left at around 14 or 15. They were patronized by lower middle-class parents, such as small tradesmen, shopkeepers, clerks, superior artisans and small tenant farmers. They did not want their children to attend an ordinary elementary school for status reasons; they preferred to rely instead on private schools and some of the smaller, less ambitious, endowed schools.

HIGHER-GRADE SCHOOLS

Once the different categories of middle-class schooling had been established, efforts were made to tackle some of the problems highlighted. A shortage of third-grade schools was partially met when some larger school boards, mainly in the industrial north of England, established 'higher-grade' schools. They were intended for elementary pupils who wished to stay on to take the fifth and higher standards of the School Code and perhaps then to study modern languages, mathematics and science. The initiative was opposed by some school board members who argued that it would encourage working-class children to move from manual work and enter offices. Nevertheless, by the mid-1890s three higher-grade schools were set up in London and 60 outside the capital.

SPORTING INTERESTS

An interest in sport in public schools spread to ambitious middle-class grammar schools, although they were frequently hampered by lack of playing space, except for drill and gymnastics. However, by the end of the 19th century, many middle-class schools had new playing fields, intended both to improve the health of the pupils and reap the moral and community benefits that team sports were believed to bestow. Indeed a criticism levelled at higher-grade schools was their lack of 'corporate life'; they needed to combine 'public school feeling … with higher grade elementary work'. The problem was mitigated where it was possible to organize 'games, such as football and cricket'.

THE PUBLIC SCHOOLS

▲ *Keats' Lane, Eton College, 1895.* This painting by George Moore Henton depicts formally attired boys at the college in the late-Victorian era: even today they still wear traditional formal dress. Lord Willoughby de Broke, who attended in the 1880s, claimed that 'no old Etonian has ever been heard to regret that he was at Eton'.

For the children of the aristocracy and gentry – the country's social and political elite – attendance at a fee-paying public school was the norm for the boys. Newly rich industrialists and well-to-do professional families saw such an education for their sons as a means by which they could penetrate elite society.

The public schools, with their curriculum centred on classical studies – Latin and Greek were the essential 'hallmark of a gentleman' – and, to a lesser extent, mathematics, had close links to Oxford and Cambridge Universities. On leaving school, many pupils attended Oxford or Cambridge whose adherence to the classics helped to maintain their central importance in the public schools' curriculum.

At the beginning of Queen Victoria's reign, however, the reputation of the public schools was at a low ebb; they were castigated for their poor moral tone, bullying and unsatisfactory academic record. Yet by 1864, when a Royal Commission reported upon the nine oldest of them, they were being extolled as 'the chief nurseries of our statesmen'.

REFORMS

Substantial reforms had begun some years earlier with the appointment of a new generation of headmasters, of whom Thomas Arnold at Rugby was perhaps the best known. Discipline was improved, better board and lodgings supplied and a new emphasis was placed upon religion. However, at Winchester, bullying and beatings by the prefects without any master's knowledge still occurred, mostly 'for dereliction of fagging duties', whereby junior boys waited on the prefects, performed valeting duties and ran errands. Nonetheless, by the mid-1860s public confidence in the schools was revived, with a new and expanding sector of the affluent middle-classes attracted to them. At the

▲ Winton House Preparatory School cricket XI in July 1869. Team games were often difficult to organize at preparatory schools because of their relatively low pupil numbers.

▼ The first chemical laboratory at Dean Close Memorial School, Cheltenham, completed in 1889. Its small size does not detract from its pioneering contribution to a public school curriculum. The master, T.M.A. Cooper, also taught mathematics.

same time, with the increase in family size, the old system of tutoring boys at home, except for the very youngest, became impractical. In addition, the transport revolution that followed the building of the railways made attendance at the schools feasible for pupils travelling from a distance.

NEW SCHOOLS

These developments led to the creation of new public schools. They included former grammar schools, such as Repton and Uppingham, which converted themselves into public schools, offering boarding facilities and the classical curriculum required to enter Oxford and Cambridge Universities. Among the new schools were proprietary establishments, proving more flexible academically than their predecessors by offering 'modern' subjects alongside the classics. At Cheltenham College, opened in 1841, it was claimed by the early 1860s that almost half of its 600 pupils were on the 'modern' side. At Harrow and Rugby, modern departments were formed to meet the needs of those wishing to pursue a military career by entering Sandhurst or Woolwich, or to enter the civil service.

Some new schools were set up from an overtly religious motive. From 1847 Canon Woodard promoted new public schools in Sussex based on High Anglican principles; the first, Lancing, opened in 1848. The Evangelical wing of the Church, alarmed at what it saw as a growing Romish tendency in the public schools, responded by creating its own establishments, including Dean Close Memorial School, opened in 1886 in Cheltenham. Dean Close also appealed to an expanding clientele by offering an engineering class for boys wishing to enter an engineering college or firm.

PLAY UP AND PLAY THE GAME

Games had always been played but they had largely been organized by the boys. At Harrow, where there was an early enthusiasm for cricket, the boys

➤ Winton House Preparatory School pupils participating in mock rifle practice with improvised rifles in the late 1860s. It was a reaction to the rifle corps being formed in many public schools.

themselves rented an additional field on which to play, and for a time they also rented a football ground until the headmaster took responsibility for it. Nevertheless, before 1850 there was no great pressure to take up sport. Some boys spent their weekly half-day holiday going for walks, fishing or joining in more juvenile pursuits with hoops, tops, quoits and marbles.

From mid-century, however, attitudes changed. Games began to be seen not merely as beneficial to health and countering idleness but as a way of imposing discipline, invoking a team spirit, and creating patriotic ideals. They were also deemed to combat any effeminate tendencies. As the 1864 Royal Commission on the Public Schools expressed it: 'The cricket and football fields ... are not merely places of exercise and amusement; they help to form some of the most valuable social qualities and manly virtues.'

The disciplinary aspect of sport manifested itself in 1853 at newly established Marlborough, when pupil revolts and poaching exploits reduced it to near bankruptcy and virtual anarchy. A new headmaster took charge and he used organized games to build team spirit, curb insubordination and end the previous disorder.

Although by the 1860s the boys still arranged much of their own sporting activity, masters now gave

them active support. At Eton, where rowing was all-important, the 'head of boats' was considered 'the greatest man in the school'; next to him ranked the captain of the cricket XI. In this new era of patriotic spirit and the manly vigour that sport imparted – what was called 'muscular Christianity' – long hours were spent in team practice, and success in inter-school matches was a source of pride. Even victories in inter-House matches were applauded: at Eton in the early 1880s, Lord Willoughby de Broke recalled the strong team spirit in his House which enabled them to win cricket and football matches against other Houses: 'One year we won the House cricket cup ... and this I put down to each one of us playing for the side.'

Military drill was also introduced into many public schools. Some set up a cadet corps or rifle club to develop the boys' shooting skills and their ability to command, setting them in good stead for future military careers.

THE CRICKET-FIELD OF LIFE

In the 1870s, F.W. Farrar, Master of Marlborough College, declared: 'No-one can make a first rate cricketer if he is not ready and steady and quick and bold ... You want the very same good qualities on the great cricket-field of life.'

DIFFERENT FOR GIRLS

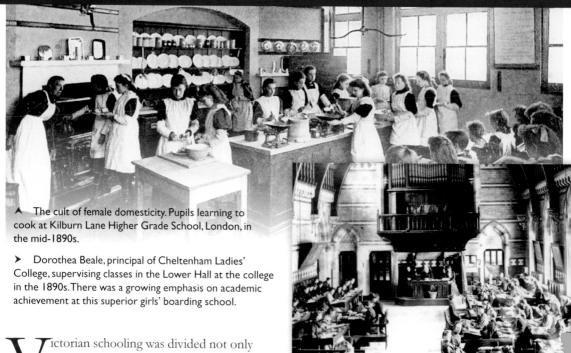

▲ The cult of female domesticity. Pupils learning to cook at Kilburn Lane Higher Grade School, London, in the mid-1890s.

➤ Dorothea Beale, principal of Cheltenham Ladies' College, supervising classes in the Lower Hall at the college in the 1890s. There was a growing emphasis on academic achievement at this superior girls' boarding school.

Victorian schooling was divided not only along class lines but also by gender. For girls, education had a moral role, to fit them for future domesticity, and, significantly, while educational reformers refined that aim they did not challenge it. As one pioneering headmistress told her school leavers, they must 'take up all necessary domestic duties – above all, … each must do humbly and faithfully the first, small, … quiet duty that lies close to her'.

For working-class pupils in elementary schools, the 1862 Revised Code made needlework compulsory. From 1874 domestic economy became a grant-earning subject, although not compulsory, while grants were offered for cookery in 1882 and for laundry work in 1890.

Fewer girls than boys attended higher grade schools. In some places elementary schoolgirls were excluded from competing for local authority scholarships; in others up to three-quarters of the awards were allocated to boys. The aim was to train girls for marriage and motherhood and as potential domestic servants.

For middle- and upper-class girls the social aspect dominated their schooling, to fit them for a suitable marriage. Coupled with this was anxiety to safeguard their superior status. In Devon in the mid-1890s it was said the 'dominant idea about girls' education is … that [they] should be kept from any contamination with people who drop their Hs or earn their salt'. Consequently many well-to-do girls were educated at home by a governess, perhaps followed by a brief spell at a prestigious European finishing school to give a little extra social polish. Others attended small private schools where the lower orders were firmly excluded, and subjects like Latin, mathematics and science were considered unfeminine and likely to deter potential suitors.

A NEW TREND

However, by mid-century those perceptions were being modified, partly because of a surplus of women in the population and with many not marrying until they were in their later 20s.

'We have a large number of girls of 13, 14, or 15 who come to us who can scarcely do the simplest sum in arithmetic ... I think that such education as they get is almost entirely showy and superficial; a little music, a little singing, a little French, a little ornamental work, and nothing else, because many girls come to us who fancy they can speak French and play the piano, but have comparatively no knowledge of English or arithmetic.'

Miss F.M. Buss to the Schools' Inquiry Commission, 30 November 1865

This meant more females had to earn a living and a better education would facilitate that. The new trend was recognized in 1848 when Queen's College was opened in London with the object of instructing potential governesses and future teachers. Alongside this, a few academically ambitious schools were being set up in the 1850s. They included Miss Buss's North London Collegiate School and the Cheltenham Ladies' College. The latter signalled its genteel credentials by excluding the daughters of tradespeople.

Miss Buss and Miss Beale, who became principal of Cheltenham Ladies' College in 1858, both wished to introduce a more rigorous curriculum but, when even the teaching of arithmetic was deemed suspect, they had to proceed cautiously.

One father complained that if his daughters 'were going to be bankers, it would be very well to teach arithmetic ... but really there is no need!' When Miss Beale introduced science into the programme it was called physical geography since this was less controversial. Later she persuaded parents that well-educated daughters would make better wives and mothers, able to help their husbands and to run their households efficiently.

The general weaknesses in female education were highlighted by the 1864–67 Schools' Inquiry Commission, which deplored the preoccupation with 'showy' accomplishments rather than more academic subjects. In consequence the 1869 Endowed Schools Act resulted in some funds being diverted to create endowed schools for girls.

∧ A botany lesson in the college museum at Cheltenham Ladies' College, c.1895.

∧ Gymnastics at Cheltenham Ladies' College in 1890, when sporting activities for girls were becoming accepted.

◄ Demure middle-class girls going for a walk from their private school in the 1890s. Parents often chose small, private establishments that concentrated on teaching 'accomplishments', such as French, art or poetry.

They were to follow the stricter intellectual regime pioneered by Miss Buss at the North London Collegiate School and, by 1894, 80 endowed schools for girls were open.

The Schools' Inquiry Commission also inspired the creation of the Girls' Public Day School Company in 1872 to fund proprietary high schools. In 1883 the Anglican Church School Company was formed on a similar basis. By 1894, jointly they were educating nearly 10,000 pupils, with the chairman of the Girls' Public Day School Company proudly describing his schools as the 'Eton and Harrow' of the female educational world. Some critics claimed that the mental strain associated with academic studies would harm the girls and damage their reproductive system. One girl who attended Oxford High School in the 1870s ironically recalled the lengthy debates: 'Skulls were measured, brains weighed, nerves tested, and conclusions were usually accompanied by warnings.'

Despite the reformers' efforts, private establishments survived alongside the new girls' schools. In 1895 there were an estimated 10,000 to 15,000 private day and boarding schools in England. As one spokeswoman said, there was an 'urgent need' to 'provide secondary schools for girls in the vast areas in which their education is left to … private adventure schools, which may or may not be sufficient to the need'. That ambition was achieved only in the 20th century.

SPORTS FOR GIRLS

For middle-class girls, sport was initially considered unsuitable, except for callisthenics, a gentle form of gymnastics, and, at boarding schools, regulation walks. But as medical evidence showed the poor health of many girls, attitudes softened. Miss Beale at Cheltenham disliked the idea of girls indulging in 'masculine' sports with their competitive edge, but when she realized that the introduction of games was inevitable, she relented.

Tennis courts were available from the 1870s and a hockey field was acquired by the early 1890s. When Miss Beale saw her first hockey match she reputedly demanded more balls to be supplied, declaring: 'The children will hurt themselves if they all run about after one ball.'

Other girls' schools were bolder. At Roedean, the first 1885 prospectus included an undertaking that to prevent over-work 'two or three hours daily will be allotted to outdoor exercise or games'. And at Southport in the mid-1890s one boarding school not only offered tennis and hockey but a 'boating club with an annual regatta'. At Worcester High School the headmistress allowed the younger girls to form a cricket club, but once girls turned 14 she said they must 'cultivate delicate, womanly refinement' rather than the 'romping vulgarity of the hoyden'.

➤ A hockey match at Cheltenham Ladies' College, c.1898.

EDUCATION'S EVOLUTION

During Queen Victoria's long reign many educational improvements were achieved and since that time the education system in Britain has continued to evolve. By 1900 there were 34,300 elementary schools being inspected in the UK, with an average of 154 pupils in each and around 42 pupils per teacher, which compares with around 21 pupils per teacher in primary schools today. The school leaving age was raised to 14 in 1918, 15 in 1947 and 16 in 1973, and government debates continue about increasing it further still. The 1944 Education Act saw the introduction of the tripartite system (grammar schools, secondary modern schools and secondary technical schools) and pupils sat the 11-plus examination for the first time; those who passed it won a place at a grammar school. Free school milk was also introduced that year, and all children received one-third of a pint (0.15 litre), until the scheme was withdrawn in 1971. In 1966 the controversial phasing out of grammar schools began, though several still remain today.

The 1988 Education Act saw the introduction of the National Curriculum; essential subjects for 5–16 year olds today, in most instances, are English, mathematics, science, ICT (information and communication technology) and PE (physical education). In more recent years several schools opted for a publicly-funded independent status and were rebranded as 'academies'.

The Victorian children who faced hunger, disease, harsh discipline and a restricted curriculum could not have begun to imagine the inviting classrooms, university-trained teachers, wide range of subjects and extra-curricular activities, nutritious school dinners, sports facilities, school trips, and the abundance of books and all kinds of technology enjoyed by their modern-day counterparts.

▼ A 'Swedish Drill' exercise class at Morning Lane Girls' School, London, in 1892. The banner bears the slogan 'A Sound Mind in a Sound Body.'

PLACES TO VISIT

Some Victorian school buildings are still in use in the 21st century, and several museums have displays on Victorian school life. Here are details of a selection of places open to visitors. Check their websites for further details, including opening dates and times.

Armley Mills Industrial Museum, Armley Park Road, Leeds, West Yorkshire LS12 2QF

Balsall Heath Victorian Classroom, c/o St Paul's Community Project Ltd, Hertford Street, Balsall Heath, Birmingham, West Midlands B12 8NJ

Beamish: the Living Museum of the North, Beamish, County Durham DH9 ORG

Black Country Museum, Tipton Road, Dudley, West Midlands DY1 4SQ

Bradford Industrial Museum, Moorside Mills, Moorside Road, Eccleshill, Bradford, West Yorkshire BD2 3HP

British Schools Museum, 41/42 Queen Street, Hitchin, Hertfordshire SG4 9TS

The Chilvers Coton Heritage Centre, Avenue Road, Nuneaton, Warwickshire CV11 4LU

Dean Heritage Centre, Camp Mill, Soudley, Forest of Dean, Gloucestershire GL14 2UB

The Old Donnison School, Church Walk, East End, Sunderland, Tyne & Wear SR1 2BN

Foundling Museum, 40 Brunswick Square, London WC1N 1AZ

Great Cressingham Victorian School, The Street, Great Cressingham, Norfolk IP25 6NL

Guildford Museum, Castle Arch, Guildford, Surrey GU1 3SX

Helston Folk Museum Victorian Schoolroom Project, Market Place, Helston, Cornwall TR13 8TH

Ironbridge Gorge Museum: Blists Hill Victorian Town, Legges Way, Madeley, Telford, Shropshire TF7 5DU

The Judge's Lodging, Broad Street, Presteigne, Powys, Mid Wales LD8 2AD

Morwellham Quay, Morwellham, Tavistock, Devon PL19 8JL

Museum of Childhood, 42 High Street, Edinburgh, Scotland EH1 1TG

Museum of Eton Life, Eton College, Eton, Windsor, Berkshire SL4 6DW

Park Hall Victorian School & Museum, Park Hall Farm, Burma Road, Oswestry, Shropshire SY11 4AS

Ragged School Museum, 46–50 Copperfield Road, London E3 4RR

Reading Museum: Victorian Schoolroom, Blagrave Street, Reading, Berkshire RG1 1QH

Rural Life Centre, Reeds Road, Tilford, Farnham, Surrey, GU10 2DL

St Fagan's National History Museum, Cardiff Road, Cardiff, South Wales CF5 6XB

St John's House Museum, St John's, Warwick, Warwickshire CV34 4NF

Sevington Victorian School, Sevington, Grittleton, Chippenham, Wiltshire SN14 7LD

Shugborough Hall County Museum, Shugborough Estate, Stafford, Staffordshire ST17 0XB

Sudbury Hall and the National Trust Museum of Childhood, Sudbury, Derbyshire DE6 5HT

Tiverton Museum of Mid Devon Life, Becks Square, Tiverton, Devon, EX16 6PJ

V&A Museum of Childhood, Cambridge Heath Road, London E2 9PA

Weald & Downland Open Air Museum, Chichester, West Sussex PO18 0EU

Weaver Hall Museum and Workhouse, 162 London Road, Northwich, Cheshire CW9 8AB

West Somerset Rural Life Museum, The Old School, Minehead, Somerset TA24 8HN

Wilderspin National School, Queen Street, Barton upon Humber, Lincolnshire DN18 5QP

The Workhouse, Upton Road, Southwell, Nottinghamshire NG25 0PT

Information correct at time of going to press.